W9-BVI-842

How Do Animals Help Make Soil?

by Ellen Lawrence

Consultant:

Shawn W. Wallace
Department of Earth and Planetary Sciences
American Museum of Natural History
New York, New York

BEARPORT
PUBLISHING

New York, New York

Credits

Cover, © Santia/Shutterstock; 4–5, © Ozgur Coskun/Shutterstock; 6, © PHOTO FUN/Shutterstock; 7, © Adam Seward/Imagebroker/FLPA; 8, © Andrea Jones Images/Alamy; 9, © Derek Middleton/FLPA; 10, © Derek Middleton/FLPA; 11, © blackeagleEMJ/Shutterstock; 12, © Malcolm Schuyl/FLPA; 13, © john michael evan potter/Shutterstock; 14, © Kampol Taepanich/Shutterstock; 15, © Lori Labrecque/Shutterstock; 16T, © Alfonso de Tomas/Shutterstock; 16BL, © blickwinkel/Alamy; 16BR, © SCIMAT/Science Photo Library; 17, © Eye of Science/Science Photo Library; 18, © Alex Fieldhouse/Alamy; 19, © Mark Moffett/Minden Pictures/FLPA; 20T, © Bill Brooks/Alamy; 20B, © BGSmith/Shutterstock; 21, © Bildagentur Zoonar Gmbh/Shutterstock; 21T, © sauletas/Shutterstock; 22, © Ruby Tuesday Books; 23TL, © CHAINFOTO24/Shutterstock; 23TC, © David Lade/Shutterstock; 23TR, © SCIMAT/Science Photo Library; 23BL, © Alexander Raths/Shutterstock; 23BC, © Alexander Raths/Shutterstock; 23BR, © redmal/iStock.

Publisher: Kenn Goin
Senior Editor: Joyce Tavolacci
Creative Director: Spencer Brinker
Design: Emma Randall
Photo Researcher: Ruby Tuesday Books Ltd

Library of Congress Cataloging-in-Publication Data

Lawrence, Ellen, 1967– author.
 How do animals help make soil? / by Ellen Lawrence.
    pages cm. — (Down & dirty : the secrets of soil)
 Summary: "In this book readers will learn how animals help make soil."— Provided by publisher.
 Audience: Ages 4–8.
 Includes bibliographical references and index.
 ISBN 978-1-62724-835-8 (library binding) — ISBN 1-62724-835-8 (library binding)
 1. Soil science—Juvenile literature. 2. Soil formation—Juvenile literature. I. Title.
 S591.3.L38 2016
 631.4—dc23
                          2015015255

For more information, write to Bearport Publishing Company, Inc., 45 West 21st Street, Suite 3B, New York, New York 10010. Printed in the United States of America.

10 9 8 7 6 5 4 3 2 1

Contents

What Lives in a Garden?

Take a look at this garden.

Many different plants grow in the soil.

Thousands of animals such as worms and ants live here, too.

These animals don't just live in the soil, though.

They also help make new soil and keep it healthy for plants.

Most plants need water, air, and **nutrients** to grow. They take these things in from the soil with their **roots**.

Making Soil from Dead Plants

Garden soil is made of bits of rock and dead plants.

Some animals help turn dead plants into soil.

How do they do this?

A wood louse is a tiny creature that eats rotting leaves, fruit, and wood.

As it feeds, it shreds dead plant material into tiny pieces that become part of the soil.

a wood louse eating dead leaves

Millipedes are small animals that have hundreds of legs! They eat rotting leaves. When they go to the bathroom, their leafy poop becomes part of the soil.

millipede

What other long, thin animals do you think play an important part in turning dead plants into soil?

Earthworms Get to Work

Another animal that turns dead plants into soil is the earthworm.

A worm feeds on dead plant material such as leaves, flowers, and fruit.

It also eats some soil.

Then, inside the worm's long body, something very important happens.

earthworm

A worm has a long, thin body and no legs. It spends most of its life underground. Although a worm's body is soft, it can push itself through hard soil using tiny hairs on its body.

Worms and Soil

A worm's meal of dead plants and soil gets mixed up inside its body.

This muddy mixture comes out of the worm's tail end as poop, or **castings**.

The castings then become part of the soil.

Worm castings are filled with nutrients that help plants grow.

So worms help turn dead plants into food for living plants!

castings

In an area of soil the size of a football field, there may be one million worms. Together, they can produce about 700 pounds (317.5 kg) of castings each day!

Many larger animals help add nutrients to soil. How do you think they do this?

Making Soil with Poop

Poop from other animals can also become part of the soil.

Cows, sheep, and horses leave piles of waste in fields.

Foxes, squirrels, and birds leave droppings on the forest floor.

All of this poop rots and adds lots of nutrients to the soil.

a woodpecker throwing poop out of its nest

ball of elephant dung

dung beetle

Dung beetles are insects that feed on the poop of other animals. Some dung beetles roll the dung they find into balls. Then they bury the dung balls in the ground to feed on later. Often, however, they don't eat all the dung and it becomes part of the soil.

Part of the Soil

Animals also help make soil by becoming part of it.

When an animal dies, its body lies on the ground.

Over time, the dead body breaks apart and rots, or **decomposes**.

Tiny pieces of flesh, feathers, fur, and bone become part of the soil.

These rotting bits add nutrients to the soil.

decomposing pigeon

a wolf feeding on a dead deer

Animals big and small help a dead body decompose. Large meat eaters such as wolves and bears tear a body into small pieces as they feed. Then tiny insects such as beetles break the remains down into smaller pieces.

Billions of Microbes

Tiny living things called **microbes** also help make soil.

A handful of soil is home to billions of microbes.

They are so tiny they can only be seen with a powerful **microscope**.

Microbes break down poop and dead plants and animals so they become soil.

goose

goose droppings

microbes in goose droppings

Microbes and other living things that break down dead plants, animals, and other materials are known as decomposers.

microbes in soil

Tiny Diggers

Many of the tiny animals that live in soil help plants stay healthy. How?

Ants and other insects dig underground homes and tunnels.

As they do this, they break up and loosen the soil.

When soil is soft and crumbly, plants can spread out their roots more easily.

The roots can then reach the air, water, and nutrients plants need.

an earthworm tunneling in the soil

As worms move around underground, they make tiny tunnels in the soil. Air and water collect in these tunnels.

soil dug from underground

entrance to ants' underground nest

a new plant growing in loose soil

Animals and Soil

Larger animals also help make the soil healthy for plants.

Rabbits, groundhogs, prairie dogs, and moles all dig underground homes.

They loosen and mix up the soil so nutrients get spread around.

From munching dead leaves to pooping and digging, animals are busy making soil—and keeping it healthy!

groundhog

prairie dog

Moles use their large front feet and claws to dig underground nests and tunnels. A mole can dig a tunnel that's 15 feet long (4.6 m) in just one hour!

In places where moles live, there are often small hills on the surface of the ground. How do you think the hills got there? (The answer is on page 24.)

mole

plant material

soil

sand

soil

sand

stones

soil

holes

Science Lab

Be a Worm Scientist

Make a worm garden and see how worms help make soil.

You will need:

- A pair of scissors
- A plastic two-liter soda bottle
- Duct tape
- Small stones
- Soil
- Sand
- Water
- Five worms from a garden
- Plant material such as dead leaves and grass clippings
- A plate
- A dark cloth
- A notebook and pencil

How to make a worm garden

1. Ask an adult to use scissors to cut off the top of a plastic bottle and to make six pea-sized holes in the bottom of it. Tape over any sharp edges on the top of the bottle using duct tape.

2. Put about 2 inches (5 cm) of stones in the bottle. Then add several layers of soil and sand. Pour half a cup of water into the bottle.

3. Place five worms on the top layer of soil. Cover them with about 1 inch (2.5 cm) of plant material.

4. Put the bottle on a plate in case any water leaks out. Place it somewhere cool, and cover it with a dark cloth. Check on your worms every few days. If the soil looks dry, add half a cup of water to it. Add more plant material as needed.

   - **What do you observe is happening to the plant material?**
   - **What do you notice about the layers of sand and soil?**

5. Write down your observations in your notebook. After two weeks, put the worms back where you found them.

22

Science Words

castings (KAST-ingz) worm waste that is passed out of an earthworm's body after it eats

decomposes (dee-kuhm-POZE-iz) rots away or decays

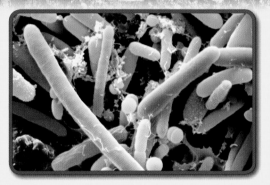

microbes (MYE-krohbz) extremely tiny living things that can only be seen with a microscope

microscope (MYE-kruh-skohp) a tool used to see things that are too small to see with the eyes alone

nutrients (NOO-tree-uhnts) vitamins, minerals, and other substances needed by living things, such as plants, to grow and be healthy

roots (ROOTS) parts of a plant that take in water and food from the soil

Index

Read More

Phillips, Dee. *Groundhog's Burrow (The Hole Truth!: Underground Animal Life).* New York: Bearport (2012).

Rockwood, Leigh. *Worms Are Gross! (Creepy Crawlies).* New York: PowerKids Press (2011).

Rosinsky, Natalie M. *Dirt: The Scoop on Soil.* North Mankato, MN: Picture Window Books (2003).

Learn More Online

To learn more about animals and soil, visit
www.bearportpublishing.com/Down&Dirty

About the Author

Ellen Lawrence lives in the United Kingdom. Her favorite books to write are those about animals and nature. In fact, the first book Ellen bought for herself, when she was six years old, was the story of a gorilla named Patty Cake that was born in New York's Central Park Zoo.

Answer for Page 21

As a mole digs a tunnel, it creates lots of loose soil underground. It then pushes all the loose soil up to the surface, forming a small pile. It's this soil that makes the hill, which is called a molehill.